Arranged by JESSE GRESS

MW00534670

THE NEEDLE AND THE DAMAGE DONE

Words and Music by
NEIL YOUNG

I caught you knockin' at my cellar door
I love you, baby, can I have some more?
Oh, the damage done
I hit the city and I lost my band
I watched the needle take another man
Gone, gone, the damage done

I sing this song because I love the man
I know that some of you don't understand
Milk blood to keep from running out
I've seen the needle and the damage done
A little part of it in everyone
But every junkie's like a settin' sun

I've seen the needle and the damage done
A little part of it in everyone
Every junkie's like a settin' sun

LIKE A HURRICANE

Words and Music by
NEIL YOUNG

Once I thought I saw you
In a crowded hazy bar
Dancin' on the light from star to star
Far across the moonbeams
I know that's who you are
I saw your brown eyes turnin' once to fire

You are like a hurricane
There's calm in your eye
And I'm gettin' blown away
To somewhere safer where the feelin' stays
I want to love you but I get so blown away

I am just a dreamer but you are just a dream
You could have been anyone to me
Before that moment you touched my lips
That perfect feeling when time just slips
Away between us on our foggy trips

You are like a hurricane
There's calm in your eye
And I'm gettin' blown away
To somewhere safer where the feeelin' stays
I want to love you but I get so blown away
Blown away

MR. SOUL

Words and Music by
NEIL YOUNG

Oh hello, Mr. Soul, I dropped by to
    pick up a reason
For the thought that I caught that my head is the
    event of the season
Why in crowds just a trace of my face could seem
    so pleasin'
I'll cop out to the change but a stranger is putting
    the tease on

I was down on a frown when the messenger
    brought me a letter
I was raised by the praise of a fan who said
    I upset her
Any girl in the world could have easily
    known me better
She said, "You're strange, but don't change"
    and I let her

In a while will the smile on my face turn to plaster?
Stick around while the clown who is sick does
    the trick of disaster
For the race of my head and my face is moving
    much faster
Is it strange I should change? I don't know,
    why don't you ask her?
Is it strange I should change? I don't know
Is it strange I should change? I don't know

THE OLD LAUGHING LADY

Words and Music by
NEIL YOUNG

Don't call pretty Peggy
She can't hear you no more
Don't leave no message
'Round her back door
They say the old laughin' lady
Been here before
She don't keep time
She don't count score

You can't have a cupboard
If there ain't no wall
You got to move
There's no time for you to stall
They say the old laughin' lady
Dropped by to call
And when she leaves
She leaves nothing at all

See the drunkard of the village
Fallin' on the street
He can't tell his ankles
From the rest of his feet
He loves his old laughin' lady
'Cause her taste is so sweet
But the laughin' lady's lovin'
Ain't the kind he can keep

There's a fever on the freeway
Blacks out the night
There's a slippin' on the stairway
Just don't feel right
There's a rumblin' in the bedroom
And a flashin' of light
There's the old laughin' lady
Everything is all right
There's the old laughin' lady
Everything is all right

TRANSFORMER MAN

Words and Music by
NEIL YOUNG

Transformer man
Transformer man

You run the show
Remote control
Direct the action with the push of a button
You're a transformer man
Power in your hand
Transformer man

Transformer man
Transformer man

Sooner or later you'll have to see
The cause and effect
So many things still left to do
But we haven't made it yet
Every morning when I look in your eyes
I feel electrified by you
Oh yeah

Transformer man
Transformer man

Transformer man
Still in command
Your eyes are shining on a beam through
    the galaxy of love
Transformer man
Unlock the secrets
Let us throw off the chains that
    keep you down

Transformer man
Transformer man

Sooner or later you'll have to see
The cause and effect
So many things still left to do
But we haven't made it yet
Every morning when I look in your eyes
I feel electrified by you
Oh yeah

Transformer man
Transformer man
Transformer man
Transformer man

LOOK OUT FOR MY LOVE

Words and Music by
NEIL YOUNG

There's a lot to learn
For wastin' time
There's a heart that burns
There's an open mind

Look out for my love
Look out for my love
Look out for my love
Look out for my love
You own it
You own it now
You own it

There's a weight on you
But you can't feel it
Livin' like I do
It's hard for you to see it
Was I hurt too bad?
Can I show you daylight?
How can I be sad
When I know that you might

Look out for my love
Look out for my love
Look out for my love
Look out for my love

Look out for my love
It's in your neighborhood
I know things are gonna change
But I can't say bad or good

Silver wings of mornin'
Shinin' in the gray day
While the ice is formin'
On a lonely runway

Hydraulic wipers pumpin'
'Til the window glistens
Somethin' sayin' somethin'
But no one seems to listen

Men with walkie-talkies
Men with flashlights waving
Up upon the tower
The clock reads daylight saving

It's home again to you, babe
You know it makes me wonder
Sittin' in the quiet slipstream
Rollin' in the thunder

Look out for my love
Look out for my love
Look out for my love
Look out for my love

Look out for my love
Look out for my love

Look out for my love
Look out for my love
Look out for my love
Look out for my love

HARVEST MOON

Words and Music by
NEIL YOUNG

Come a little bit closer
Hear what I have to say
Just like children sleepin'
We could dream this night away
But there's a full moon risin'
Let's go dancin' in the light
We know where the music's playin'
Let's go out and feel the night

Because I'm still in love with you
I want to see you dance again
Because I'm still in love with you
On this harvest moon

When we were strangers
I watched you from afar
Then when we were lovers
I loved you with all my heart
But now it's gettin' late
And the moon is climbin' high
I want to celebrate
See it shinin' in your eye

Because I'm still in love with you
I want to see you dance again
Because I'm still in love with you
On this harvest moon
Because I'm still in love with you
I want to see you dance again
Because I'm still in love with you
On this harvest moon
Because I'm still in love with you
I want to see you dance again
Because I'm still in love with you
On this harvest moon

UNKNOWN LEGEND

Words and Music by
NEIL YOUNG

She used to work in a diner
Never saw a woman look finer
I used to order just to watch her float
    across the floor
She grew up in a small town
Never put her roots down
Daddy always kept movin' so she did too

Somewhere on a desert highway
She rides a Harley-Davidson
Her long blonde hair flyin' in the wind
She's been runnin' half her life
The chrome and steel she rides
Collidin' with the very air she breathes
The air she breathes

You know it ain't easy
You got to hold on
She was an unknown legend in her time
Now she's dressin' two kids
Lookin' for a magic kiss
She gets the far-away look in her eyes

Somewhere on a desert highway
She rides a Harley-Davidson
Her long blonde hair flyin' in the wind
She's been runnin' half her life
The chrome and steel she rides
Collidin' with the very air she breathes
The air she breathes

Somewhere on a desert highway
She rides a Harley-Davidson
Her long blonde hair flyin' in the wind
She's been runnin' half her life
The chrome and steel she rides
Collidin' with the very air she breathes
The air she breathes

LONG MAY YOU RUN

Words and Music by
NEIL YOUNG

We've been through some things together
With trunks of memories still to come
We found things to do in stormy weather
Long may you run

Long may you run
Long may you run
Although these changes have come
With your chrome heart shining
In the sun
Long may you run

Well, it was back in Blind River in 1962
When I last saw you alive
But we missed that shift on the long decline
Long may you run

Long may you run
Long may you run
Although these changes have come
With your chrome heart shining
In the sun
Long may you run

Maybe The Beach Boys have got you now
With those waves singin' "Caroline No"
Rollin' down that empty ocean road
Gettin' to the surf on time

Long may you run
Long may you run
Although these changes have come
With your chrome heart shining
In the sun
Long may you run

Long may you run
Long may you run
Although these changes have come
With your chrome heart shining
In the sun
Long may you run

FROM HANK TO HENDRIX

Words and Music by
NEIL YOUNG

From Hank to Hendrix
I walked these streets with you
Here I am with this old guitar
Doin' what I do

I always expected
That you would see me through
I never believed in much
But I believed in you

Can we get it together
Can we still stand side by side
Can we make it last
Like a musical ride?

From Marilyn to Madonna
I always loved your smile
Now we're headed for the big divorce
California-style

I hear myself singin'
Like a long-lost friend.
The same thing that makes you live
Can kill you in the end

Can we get it together
Can we still stand side by side
Can we make it last
Like a musical ride?

Sometimes it's distorted
Not clear to you
Sometimes the beauty of love
Just comes ringin' through

New glass in the window
New leaf on the tree
New distance between us
You and me

Can we get it together
Can we still stand side by side
Can we make it last
Like a musical ride?

POCAHONTAS

Words and Music by
NEIL YOUNG

Aurora Borealis
The icy sky at night
Paddles cut the water
In a long and hurried flight
From the white man to the fields of green
And the homeland we've never seen

They killed us in our teepees
And they cut our women down
They might have left some babies
Cryin' on the ground
But the firesticks and the wagons come
And the night falls on the settin' sun

They massacred the buffalo
Kitty-corner from the bank
Taxis run across my feet
And my eyes have turned to blanks
In my little box at the top of the stairs
With my Indian rug and a pipe to share

I wish I was a trapper
I would give a thousand pelts
To sleep with Pocahontas
And find out how she felt
In the mornin' on the fields of green
In the homeland we've never seen

And maybe Marlon Brando
Will be there by the fire
We'll sit and talk about Hollywood
And the good things there for hire
Like the Astrodome and the first teepee
Marlon Brando. Pocahontas and me
Marlon Brando. Pocahontas and me
Pocahontas

WORLD ON A STRING

Words and Music by
NEIL YOUNG

You know I lose, you know I win
You know I called for the shape I'm in
It's just a game you see me play
Only real in the way that I feel from day to day

Although the answer is not unknown
I'm searchin', searchin', and how I've grown
It's not all right to say goodbye
And the world on a string doesn't mean a thing

No. the world on a string doesn't mean a thing
It's only real in the way that I feel from day to day
Day to day

STRINGMAN

Words and Music by
NEIL YOUNG

You can say the soul is gone
And the feelin's just not there
Not like it was so long ago
On the empty page before you
You can fill in what you care
Try to make it new before you go

Take the simple case of the sarge
Who wouldn't go back to war
'Cause the hippies tore down everything
   that he was fightin' for
Or the lovers on the blankets
The city turned to whores
With memories of green kissed by the sun

You can say the soul is gone
And close another door
Just be sure that yours is not the one

And I'm singin' for the stringman
Who lately lost his wife
There is no dearer friend of mine
That I know in this life
On his shoulder rests a violin
For his head where chaos reigns
But his heart can't find a simple way
To live with all those things
All those things
He's a stringman
A stringman
All those strings to pull

HELPLESS

Words and Music by
NEIL YOUNG

There is a town in north Ontario
With dream comfort memory despair
And in my mind I still need a place to go
All my changes were there

Blue, blue windows behind the stars
Yellow moon on the rise
Big birds flyin' across the sky
Throwin' shadows on our eyes
Leave us

Helpless, helpless, helpless
Well, babe, can you hear me now?
The chains are locked and tied
   across my doors
Baby, baby, sing with me somehow

Blue, blue windows behind the stars
Yellow moon on the rise
Big birds flyin' across the sky
Throwin' shadows on our eyes
Leave us

Helpless, helpless, helpless
Helpless, helpless, helpless
Helpless, helpless, helpless
Helpless, helpless, helpless

Helpless, helpless, helpless

Transcriptions edited by Joel Bernstein

CONTENTS

Key To Notation Symbols

THE OLD LAUGHING LADY

Words and Music by
NEIL YOUNG

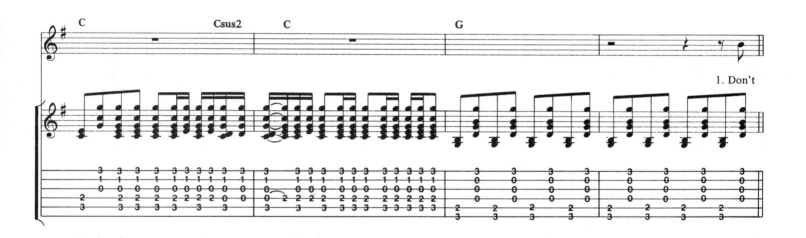

Verse 3:

3. See the drunk-ard of the vil - lage   fall - in' on _____ the

*Palm mute on strings ⑤ and ⑥

There's the old laugh-in' la-dy, ev-'ry-thing is all right.

MR. SOUL

**Words and Music by
NEIL YOUNG**

WORLD ON A STRING

Words and Music by
NEIL YOUNG

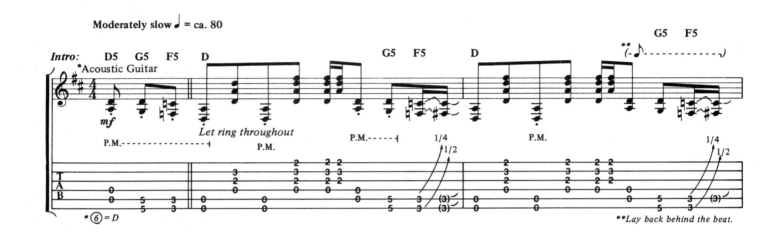

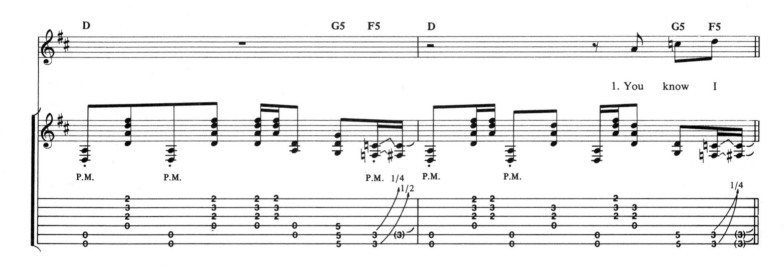

POCAHONTAS

Words and Music by
NEIL YOUNG

*Palm mute on string 6.   **Palm mute on strings 5 and 6.

(Harmonica solo:)

4. I wish I was____ a trap - per. I would

Verse 4:

**Palm mute on strings 5 and 6.

**Palm mute on strings 5 and 6.

(Harmonica solo:)

Verse 5:

5. And may - be Mar - lon Bran - do   will

be there   by   the fire.____   We'll sit   and   talk ____ a - bout

STRINGMAN

Words and Music by
NEIL YOUNG

Moderately slow ♩ = ca. 86
*Acoustic Guitar (Piano arranged for Guitar)

1. You can say the soul is gone.___

*Capo at 3rd fret ⑥ =D, ⑤ = A, ④ = D, ③ = G, ② = B, ① = E.

Let ring throughout

42

LIKE A HURRICANE

Words and Music by
NEIL YOUNG

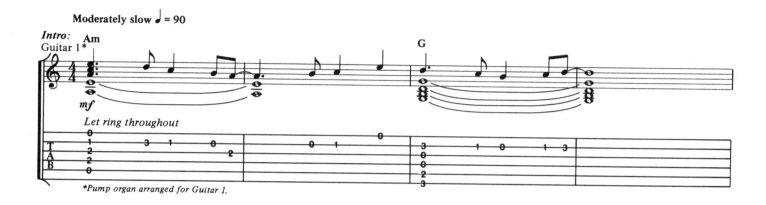

Pump organ arranged for Guitar 1.

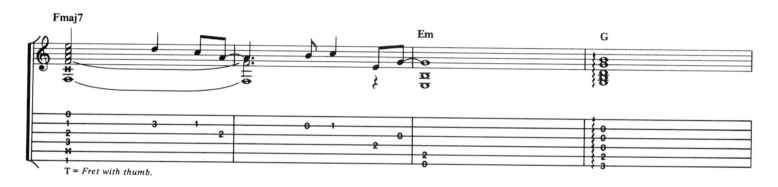

T = Fret with thumb.

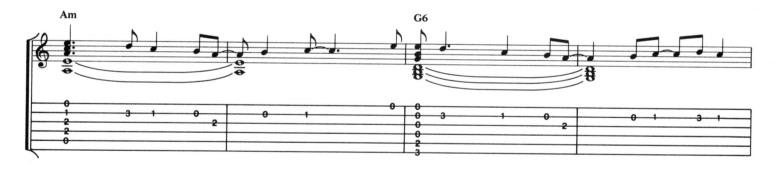

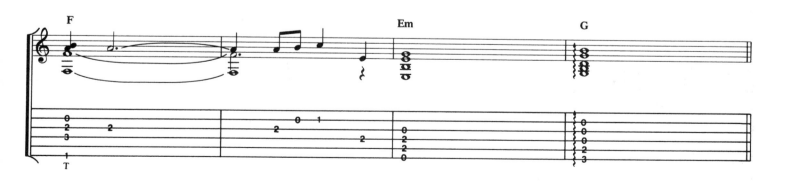

*Play this bass note (G) on Verse 2 only.

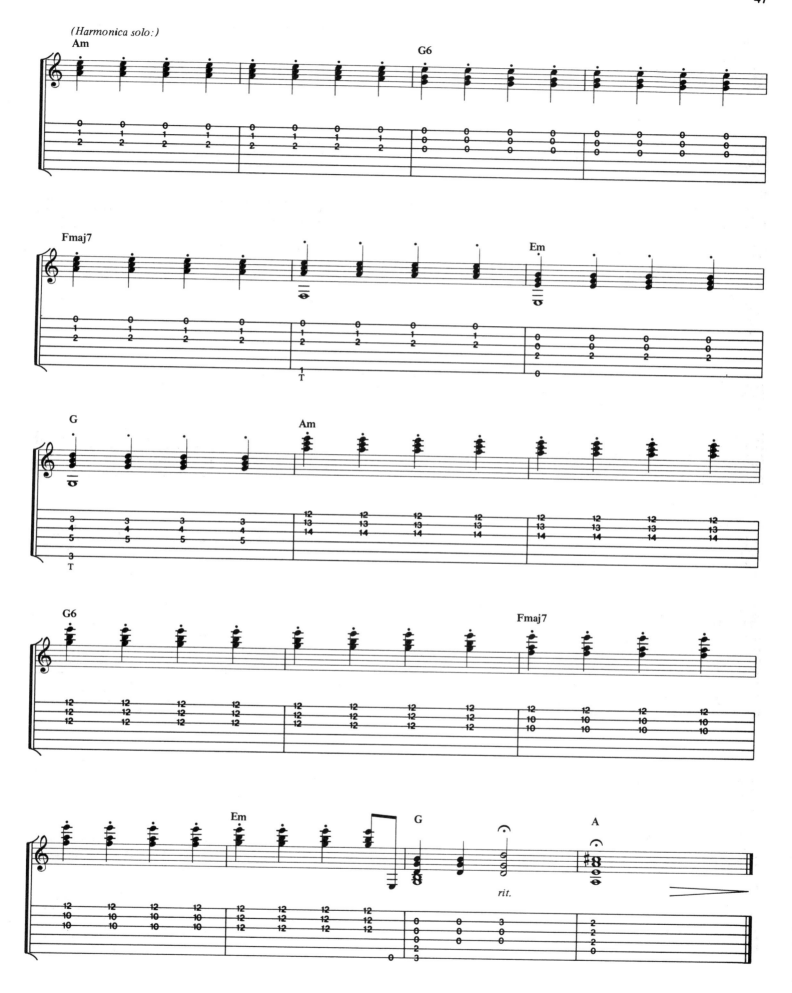

THE NEEDLE AND THE DAMAGE DONE

Words and Music by
NEIL YOUNG

50

HELPLESS

Words and Music by
NEIL YOUNG

1. There is a town in north On - tar - i - o,

ex - treme____ com - fort, mem - o - ry____ de - spair,____ and in my mind,_ I still

need_ a place_ to go,____ all_____ my chang - es were there.____

54

HARVEST MOON

Words and Music by
NEIL YOUNG

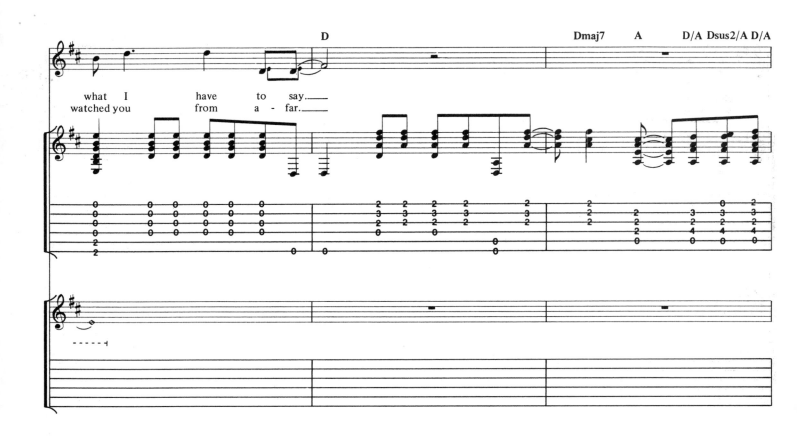

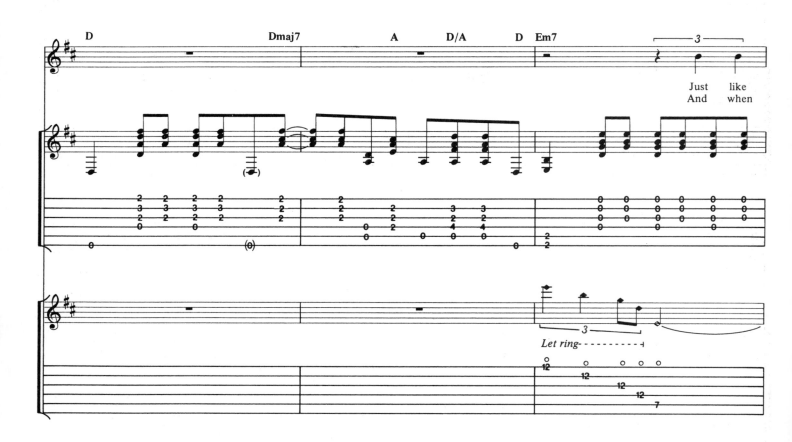

TRANSFORMER MAN

Words and Music by
NEIL YOUNG

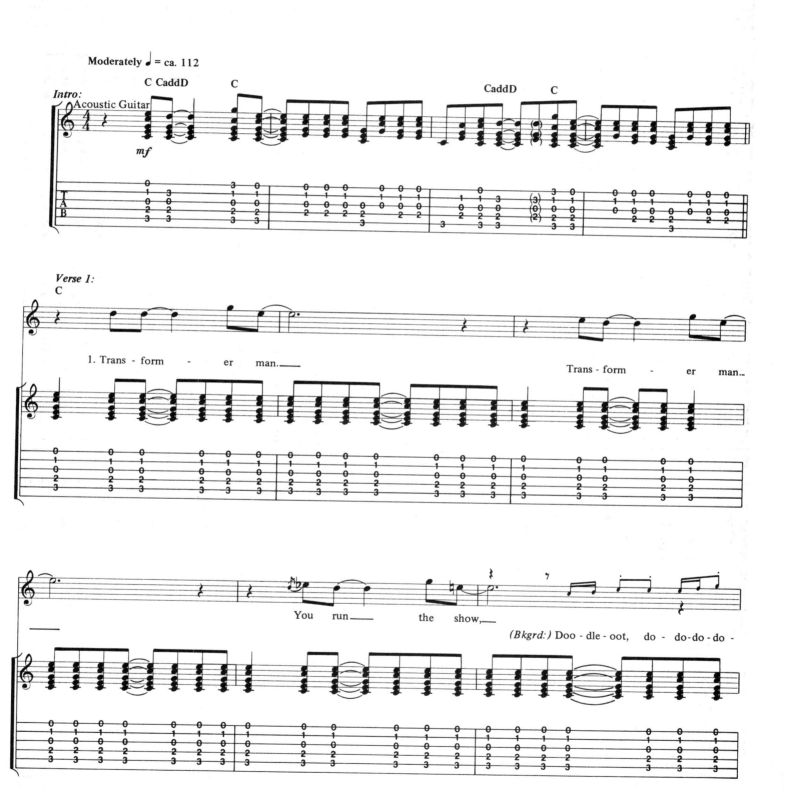

64

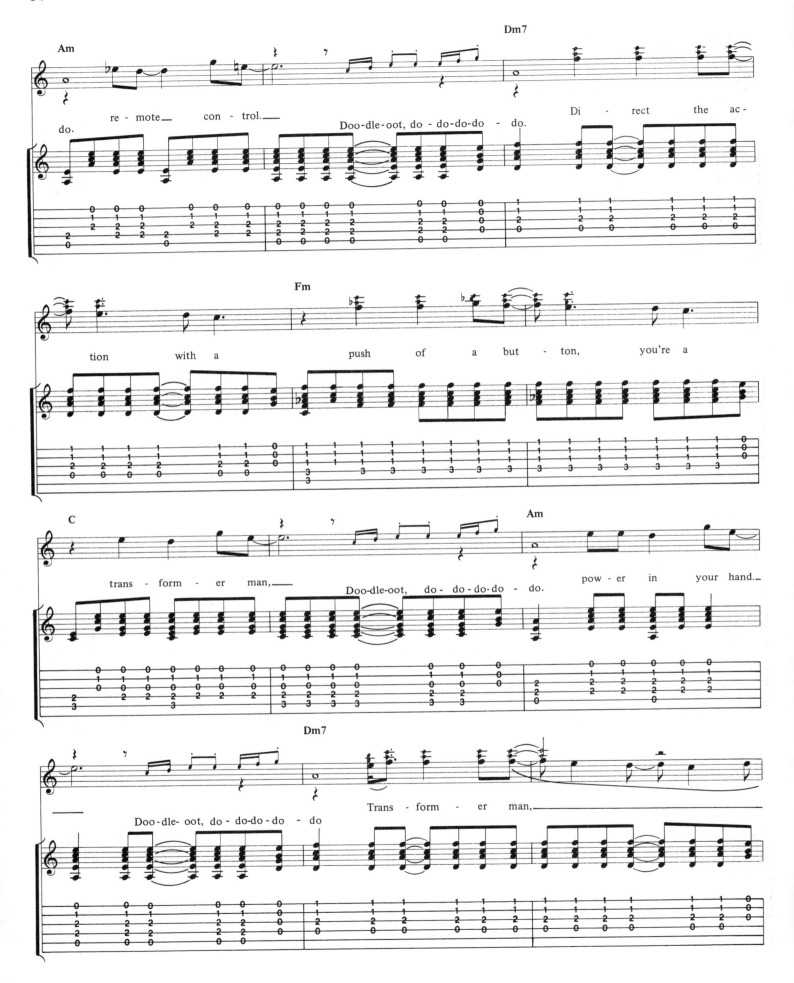

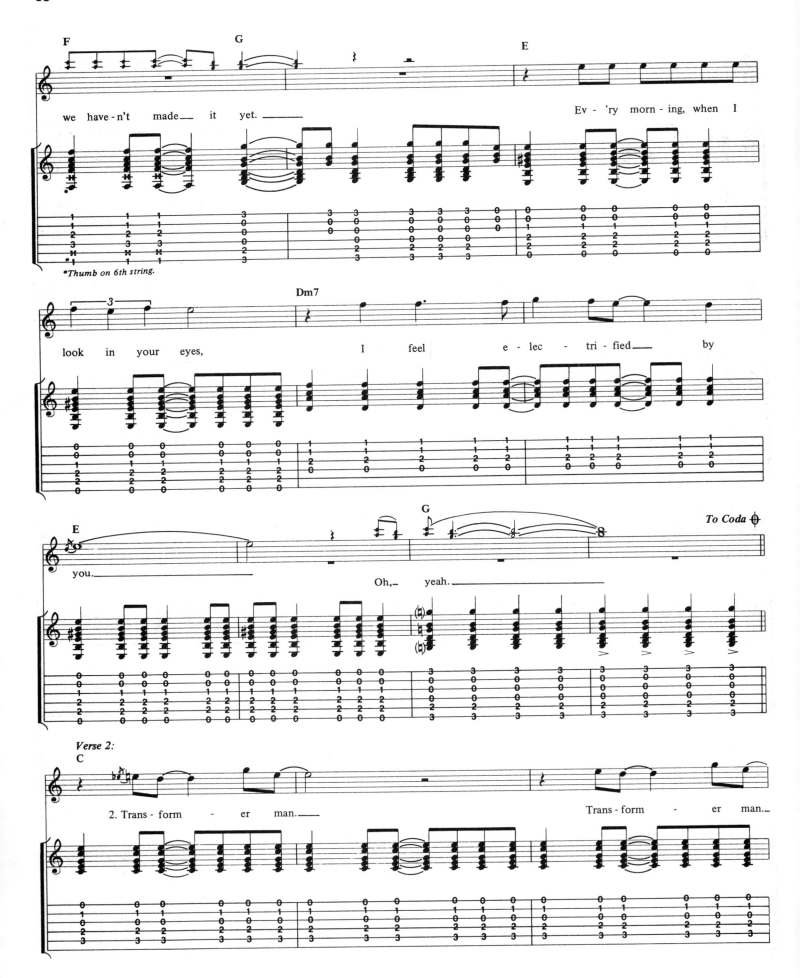

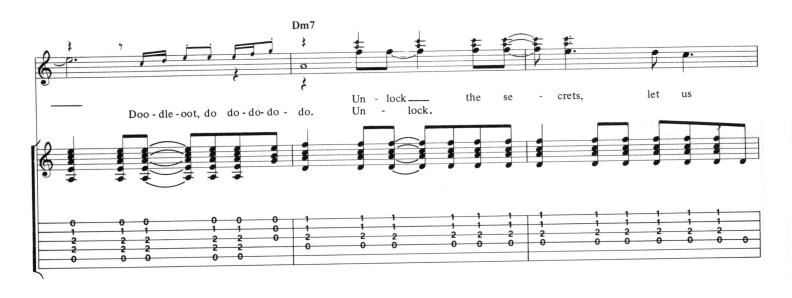

Doo - dle -oot, do do-do-do- do.
Un - lock____ the se - crets, let us
Un - lock,

throw off the chains___ that__ keep you down.___ Trans - form - er man._

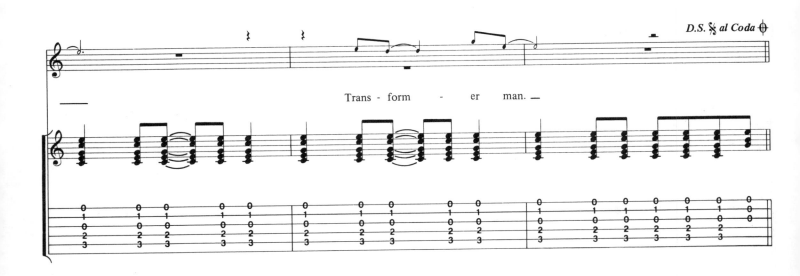

Trans - form - er man. _

D.S. 𝄋 *al Coda* ⊕

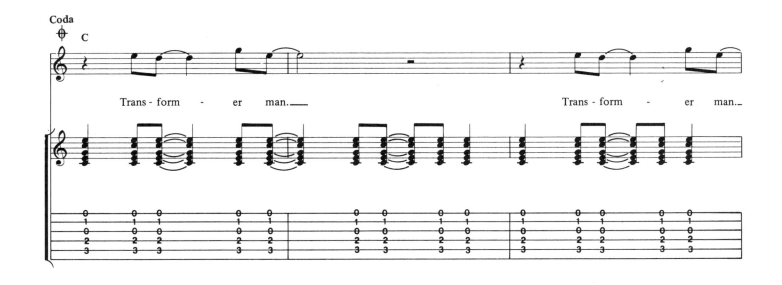

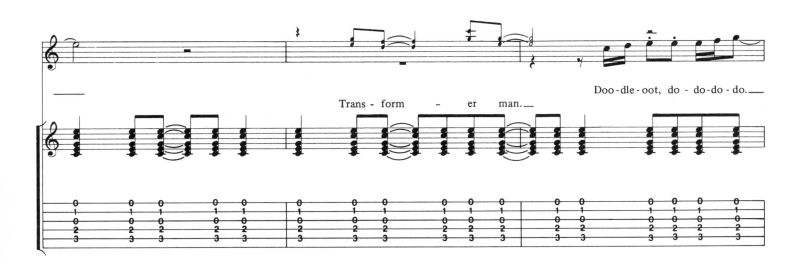

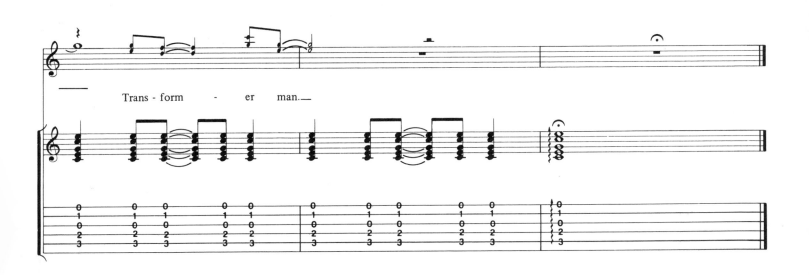

UNKNOWN LEGEND

Words and Music by
NEIL YOUNG

72

hair fly - in' in the wind._____ oo, oo._____ She's been run - nin'
(Background:)Oo,_____

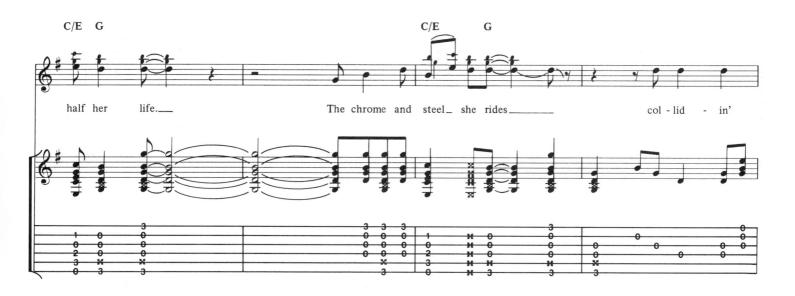

half her life.___ The chrome and steel_ she rides_____ col - lid - in'

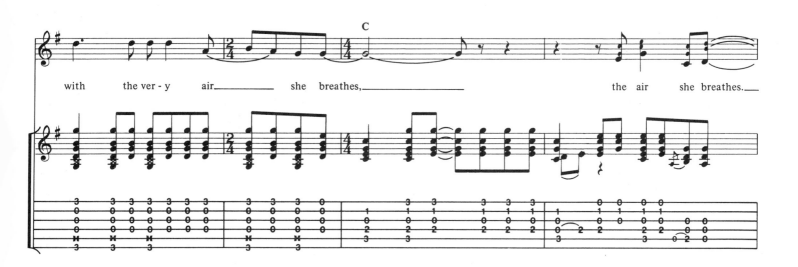

with the ver - y air_____ she breathes,_____ the air she breathes.___

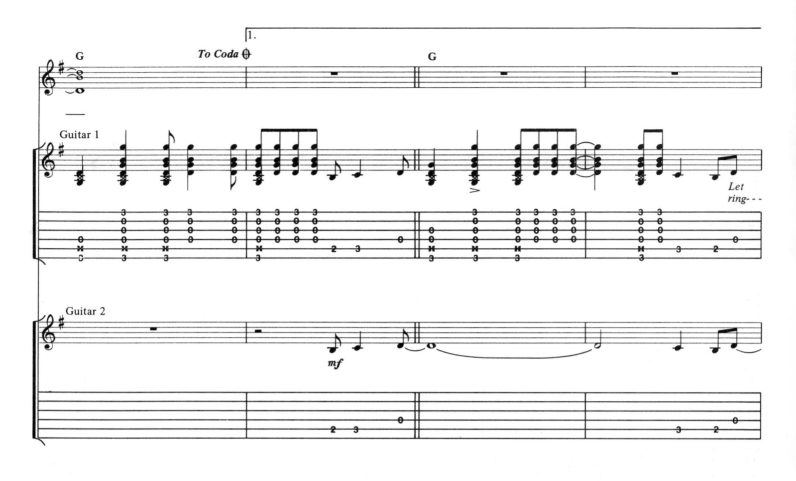

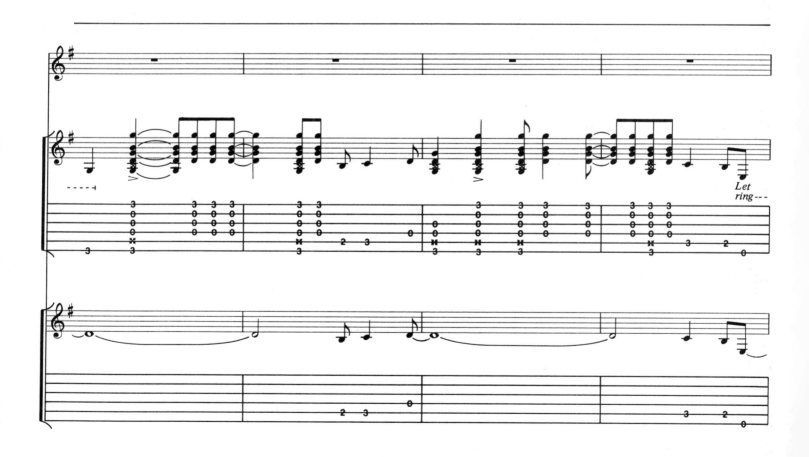

LOOK OUT FOR MY LOVE

Words and Music by
NEIL YOUNG

78

*T = fret strings 5 and 6 with thumb.

84

88

LONG MAY YOU RUN

Words and Music by
NEIL YOUNG

Additional lyrics

Verse 2: Well, it was back in Blind River in nine-teen sixty-two when I last saw you alive.
But we missed that shift on the long decline, long may you run.
(To Chorus:)

Verse 3: Maybe the Beach Boys have got you now, with those waves singin' "Caroline."
Rollin' down that empty ocean road, gettin' to the surf on time.
(To Chorus:)

FROM HANK TO HENDRIX

Words and Music by
NEIL YOUNG

96

Chorus:

Can we get it to-geth - er, can we still___ dance side by side?___

Can we make it last_____ like a mu - si - cal ride?___

Additional lyrics

Verse 2: From Marylin to Madonna, I always loved your smile.
Now we've headed for the big divorce, California style.
I found myself singin' like a long lost friend.
The same thing that makes you live can kill you in the end.

Verse 3: Sometimes it's distorted, not clear to you.
Sometimes the beauty of love just comes ringin' through.
New glass in the window, new leaf on the tree.
New distance between us, you 'n' me, you 'n' me.